MW01227072

Mom's Menu Planner

Creative Planners

Copyright © 2015 by Creative Planners

For the month of: _____

Week of: _____	MONDAY
	Breakfast: _____
	Lunch: _____
	Dinner: Instant pot Lentil soup
	Snack: _____

TUESDAY	WEDNESDAY
Breakfast: _____	Breakfast: _____
Lunch: This left over soup/Avo	Lunch: Chickpeas & Avo
Dinner: Roasted Veggies for 2 Chicken Rice Salad	Dinner: pasta w/ Broch
Snack: _____	Snack: _____

THURSDAY	FRIDAY
Breakfast: _____	Breakfast: _____
Lunch: _____	Lunch: _____
Dinner: _____	Dinner: _____
Snack: _____	Snack: _____

SATURDAY	SUNDAY
Breakfast: _____	Breakfast: _____
Lunch: _____	Lunch: _____
Dinner: _____	Dinner: _____
Snack: _____	Snack: _____

SHOPPING LIST:

For the month of: _____

Week of:

MONDAY
Breakfast: _____

Lunch: _____

Dinner: _____

Snack: _____

TUESDAY
Breakfast: _____

Lunch: _____

Dinner: _____

Snack: _____

WEDNESDAY
Breakfast: _____

Lunch: _____

Dinner: _____

Snack: _____

THURSDAY
Breakfast: _____

Lunch: _____

Dinner: _____

Snack: _____

FRIDAY
Breakfast: _____

Lunch: _____

Dinner: _____

Snack: _____

SATURDAY
Breakfast: _____

Lunch: _____

Dinner: _____

Snack: _____

SUNDAY
Breakfast: _____

Lunch: _____

Dinner: _____

Snack: _____

SHOPPING LIST:

_____ _____

_____ _____

_____ _____

_____ _____

_____ _____

_____ _____

_____ _____

For the month of: _____

Week of:
_____

MONDAY
Breakfast: _____
_____
Lunch: _____
_____
Dinner: _____
_____
Snack: _____

TUESDAY
Breakfast: _____
_____
Lunch: _____
_____
Dinner: _____
_____
Snack: _____

WEDNESDAY
Breakfast: _____
_____
Lunch: _____
_____
Dinner: _____
_____
Snack: _____

THURSDAY
Breakfast: _____
_____
Lunch: _____
_____
Dinner: _____
_____
Snack: _____

FRIDAY
Breakfast: _____
_____
Lunch: _____
_____
Dinner: _____
_____
Snack: _____

SATURDAY
Breakfast: _____
_____
Lunch: _____
_____
Dinner: _____
_____
Snack: _____

SUNDAY
Breakfast: _____
_____
Lunch: _____
_____
Dinner: _____
_____
Snack: _____

SHOPPING LIST:

_____   _____
_____   _____
_____   _____
_____   _____
_____   _____
_____   _____
_____   _____

For the month of: _____

Week of:	MONDAY
	Breakfast: _____
	Lunch: _____
	Dinner: _____
	Snack: _____

TUESDAY
Breakfast: _____

Lunch: _____

Dinner: _____

Snack: _____

WEDNESDAY
Breakfast: _____

Lunch: _____

Dinner: _____

Snack: _____

THURSDAY
Breakfast: _____

Lunch: _____

Dinner: _____

Snack: _____

FRIDAY
Breakfast: _____

Lunch: _____

Dinner: _____

Snack: _____

SATURDAY
Breakfast: _____

Lunch: _____

Dinner: _____

Snack: _____

SUNDAY
Breakfast: _____

Lunch: _____

Dinner: _____

Snack: _____

SHOPPING LIST:

_____   _____
_____   _____
_____   _____
_____   _____
_____   _____
_____   _____
_____   _____

For the month of: _____

Week of:

MONDAY
Breakfast: _____
Lunch: _____
Dinner: _____
Snack: _____

TUESDAY
Breakfast: _____
Lunch: _____
Dinner: _____
Snack: _____

WEDNESDAY
Breakfast: _____
Lunch: _____
Dinner: _____
Snack: _____

THURSDAY
Breakfast: _____
Lunch: _____
Dinner: _____
Snack: _____

FRIDAY
Breakfast: _____
Lunch: _____
Dinner: _____
Snack: _____

SATURDAY
Breakfast: _____
Lunch: _____
Dinner: _____
Snack: _____

SUNDAY
Breakfast: _____
Lunch: _____
Dinner: _____
Snack: _____

SHOPPING LIST:

For the month of: _____

Week of:	**MONDAY** Breakfast: _____ Lunch: _____ Dinner: _____ Snack: _____
TUESDAY Breakfast: _____ Lunch: _____ Dinner: _____ Snack: _____	**WEDNESDAY** Breakfast: _____ Lunch: _____ Dinner: _____ Snack: _____
THURSDAY Breakfast: _____ Lunch: _____ Dinner: _____ Snack: _____	**FRIDAY** Breakfast: _____ Lunch: _____ Dinner: _____ Snack: _____
SATURDAY Breakfast: _____ Lunch: _____ Dinner: _____ Snack: _____	**SUNDAY** Breakfast: _____ Lunch: _____ Dinner: _____ Snack: _____

SHOPPING LIST:

For the month of: _____

Week of:

MONDAY
Breakfast: _____
_____
Lunch: _____
_____
Dinner: _____
_____
Snack: _____

TUESDAY
Breakfast: _____
_____
Lunch: _____
_____
Dinner: _____
_____
Snack: _____

WEDNESDAY
Breakfast: _____
_____
Lunch: _____
_____
Dinner: _____
_____
Snack: _____

THURSDAY
Breakfast: _____
_____
Lunch: _____
_____
Dinner: _____
_____
Snack: _____

FRIDAY
Breakfast: _____
_____
Lunch: _____
_____
Dinner: _____
_____
Snack: _____

SATURDAY
Breakfast: _____
_____
Lunch: _____
_____
Dinner: _____
_____
Snack: _____

SUNDAY
Breakfast: _____
_____
Lunch: _____
_____
Dinner: _____
_____
Snack: _____

SHOPPING LIST:

_____   _____
_____   _____
_____   _____
_____   _____
_____   _____
_____   _____
_____   _____

For the month of: _____

Week of:	MONDAY
	Breakfast: _____
	Lunch: _____
	Dinner: _____
	Snack: _____

TUESDAY	WEDNESDAY
Breakfast: _____	Breakfast: _____
Lunch: _____	Lunch: _____
Dinner: _____	Dinner: _____
Snack: _____	Snack: _____

THURSDAY	FRIDAY
Breakfast: _____	Breakfast: _____
Lunch: _____	Lunch: _____
Dinner: _____	Dinner: _____
Snack: _____	Snack: _____

SATURDAY	SUNDAY
Breakfast: _____	Breakfast: _____
Lunch: _____	Lunch: _____
Dinner: _____	Dinner: _____
Snack: _____	Snack: _____

SHOPPING LIST:

For the month of: _____

Week of:	**MONDAY** Breakfast: _____ Lunch: _____ Dinner: _____ Snack: _____
TUESDAY Breakfast: _____ Lunch: _____ Dinner: _____ Snack: _____	**WEDNESDAY** Breakfast: _____ Lunch: _____ Dinner: _____ Snack: _____
THURSDAY Breakfast: _____ Lunch: _____ Dinner: _____ Snack: _____	**FRIDAY** Breakfast: _____ Lunch: _____ Dinner: _____ Snack: _____
SATURDAY Breakfast: _____ Lunch: _____ Dinner: _____ Snack: _____	**SUNDAY** Breakfast: _____ Lunch: _____ Dinner: _____ Snack: _____

SHOPPING LIST:

_____ _____
_____ _____
_____ _____
_____ _____
_____ _____
_____ _____

For the month of: _____

Week of:	**MONDAY** Breakfast: _____ Lunch: _____ Dinner: _____ Snack: _____
TUESDAY Breakfast: _____ Lunch: _____ Dinner: _____ Snack: _____	**WEDNESDAY** Breakfast: _____ Lunch: _____ Dinner: _____ Snack: _____
THURSDAY Breakfast: _____ Lunch: _____ Dinner: _____ Snack: _____	**FRIDAY** Breakfast: _____ Lunch: _____ Dinner: _____ Snack: _____
SATURDAY Breakfast: _____ Lunch: _____ Dinner: _____ Snack: _____	**SUNDAY** Breakfast: _____ Lunch: _____ Dinner: _____ Snack: _____

SHOPPING LIST:

_____   _____
_____   _____
_____   _____
_____   _____
_____   _____
_____   _____

For the month of: _____

Week of:

MONDAY
Breakfast: _____

Lunch: _____

Dinner: _____

Snack: _____

TUESDAY
Breakfast: _____

Lunch: _____

Dinner: _____

Snack: _____

WEDNESDAY
Breakfast: _____

Lunch: _____

Dinner: _____

Snack: _____

THURSDAY
Breakfast: _____

Lunch: _____

Dinner: _____

Snack: _____

FRIDAY
Breakfast: _____

Lunch: _____

Dinner: _____

Snack: _____

SATURDAY
Breakfast: _____

Lunch: _____

Dinner: _____

Snack: _____

SUNDAY
Breakfast: _____

Lunch: _____

Dinner: _____

Snack: _____

SHOPPING LIST:

For the month of: _____

Week of:

MONDAY
Breakfast: _____
Lunch: _____
Dinner: _____
Snack: _____

TUESDAY
Breakfast: _____
Lunch: _____
Dinner: _____
Snack: _____

WEDNESDAY
Breakfast: _____
Lunch: _____
Dinner: _____
Snack: _____

THURSDAY
Breakfast: _____
Lunch: _____
Dinner: _____
Snack: _____

FRIDAY
Breakfast: _____
Lunch: _____
Dinner: _____
Snack: _____

SATURDAY
Breakfast: _____
Lunch: _____
Dinner: _____
Snack: _____

SUNDAY
Breakfast: _____
Lunch: _____
Dinner: _____
Snack: _____

SHOPPING LIST:

_____   _____
_____   _____
_____   _____
_____   _____
_____   _____
_____   _____

For the month of: _____

Week of:	MONDAY
	Breakfast: _____
	Lunch: _____
	Dinner: _____
	Snack: _____

TUESDAY	WEDNESDAY
Breakfast: _____	Breakfast: _____
Lunch: _____	Lunch: _____
Dinner: _____	Dinner: _____
Snack: _____	Snack: _____

THURSDAY	FRIDAY
Breakfast: _____	Breakfast: _____
Lunch: _____	Lunch: _____
Dinner: _____	Dinner: _____
Snack: _____	Snack: _____

SATURDAY	SUNDAY
Breakfast: _____	Breakfast: _____
Lunch: _____	Lunch: _____
Dinner: _____	Dinner: _____
Snack: _____	Snack: _____

SHOPPING LIST:

_____   _____
_____   _____
_____   _____
_____   _____
_____   _____
_____   _____

For the month of: _____

Week of:	MONDAY
	Breakfast: _____
	Lunch: _____
	Dinner: _____
	Snack: _____

TUESDAY	WEDNESDAY
Breakfast: _____	Breakfast: _____
Lunch: _____	Lunch: _____
Dinner: _____	Dinner: _____
Snack: _____	Snack: _____

THURSDAY	FRIDAY
Breakfast: _____	Breakfast: _____
Lunch: _____	Lunch: _____
Dinner: _____	Dinner: _____
Snack: _____	Snack: _____

SATURDAY	SUNDAY
Breakfast: _____	Breakfast: _____
Lunch: _____	Lunch: _____
Dinner: _____	Dinner: _____
Snack: _____	Snack: _____

SHOPPING LIST:

For the month of: _____

Week of:	**MONDAY**
	Breakfast: _____
	Lunch: _____
	Dinner: _____
	Snack: _____

TUESDAY	**WEDNESDAY**
Breakfast: _____	Breakfast: _____
Lunch: _____	Lunch: _____
Dinner: _____	Dinner: _____
Snack: _____	Snack: _____

THURSDAY	**FRIDAY**
Breakfast: _____	Breakfast: _____
Lunch: _____	Lunch: _____
Dinner: _____	Dinner: _____
Snack: _____	Snack: _____

SATURDAY	**SUNDAY**
Breakfast: _____	Breakfast: _____
Lunch: _____	Lunch: _____
Dinner: _____	Dinner: _____
Snack: _____	Snack: _____

SHOPPING LIST:

_____ _____
_____ _____
_____ _____
_____ _____
_____ _____
_____ _____

For the month of: _____

Week of:	**MONDAY** Breakfast: _____ Lunch: _____ Dinner: _____ Snack: _____
TUESDAY Breakfast: _____ Lunch: _____ Dinner: _____ Snack: _____	**WEDNESDAY** Breakfast: _____ Lunch: _____ Dinner: _____ Snack: _____
THURSDAY Breakfast: _____ Lunch: _____ Dinner: _____ Snack: _____	**FRIDAY** Breakfast: _____ Lunch: _____ Dinner: _____ Snack: _____
SATURDAY Breakfast: _____ Lunch: _____ Dinner: _____ Snack: _____	**SUNDAY** Breakfast: _____ Lunch: _____ Dinner: _____ Snack: _____

SHOPPING LIST:

For the month of: _____

Week of:

MONDAY
Breakfast: _____
Lunch: _____
Dinner: _____
Snack: _____

TUESDAY
Breakfast: _____
Lunch: _____
Dinner: _____
Snack: _____

WEDNESDAY
Breakfast: _____
Lunch: _____
Dinner: _____
Snack: _____

THURSDAY
Breakfast: _____
Lunch: _____
Dinner: _____
Snack: _____

FRIDAY
Breakfast: _____
Lunch: _____
Dinner: _____
Snack: _____

SATURDAY
Breakfast: _____
Lunch: _____
Dinner: _____
Snack: _____

SUNDAY
Breakfast: _____
Lunch: _____
Dinner: _____
Snack: _____

SHOPPING LIST:

For the month of: _____

Week of:	**MONDAY** Breakfast: _____ Lunch: _____ Dinner: _____ Snack: _____
TUESDAY Breakfast: _____ Lunch: _____ Dinner: _____ Snack: _____	**WEDNESDAY** Breakfast: _____ Lunch: _____ Dinner: _____ Snack: _____
THURSDAY Breakfast: _____ Lunch: _____ Dinner: _____ Snack: _____	**FRIDAY** Breakfast: _____ Lunch: _____ Dinner: _____ Snack: _____
SATURDAY Breakfast: _____ Lunch: _____ Dinner: _____ Snack: _____	**SUNDAY** Breakfast: _____ Lunch: _____ Dinner: _____ Snack: _____

SHOPPING LIST:

For the month of: _____

Week of:	**MONDAY**
	Breakfast: _____
	Lunch: _____
	Dinner: _____
	Snack: _____

TUESDAY	**WEDNESDAY**
Breakfast: _____	Breakfast: _____
Lunch: _____	Lunch: _____
Dinner: _____	Dinner: _____
Snack: _____	Snack: _____

THURSDAY	**FRIDAY**
Breakfast: _____	Breakfast: _____
Lunch: _____	Lunch: _____
Dinner: _____	Dinner: _____
Snack: _____	Snack: _____

SATURDAY	**SUNDAY**
Breakfast: _____	Breakfast: _____
Lunch: _____	Lunch: _____
Dinner: _____	Dinner: _____
Snack: _____	Snack: _____

SHOPPING LIST:

_____ _____
_____ _____
_____ _____
_____ _____
_____ _____
_____ _____

For the month of: _____

Week of: _____

MONDAY
Breakfast: _____
_____
Lunch: _____
_____
Dinner: _____
_____
Snack: _____

TUESDAY
Breakfast: _____
_____
Lunch: _____
_____
Dinner: _____
_____
Snack: _____

WEDNESDAY
Breakfast: _____
_____
Lunch: _____
_____
Dinner: _____
_____
Snack: _____

THURSDAY
Breakfast: _____
_____
Lunch: _____
_____
Dinner: _____
_____
Snack: _____

FRIDAY
Breakfast: _____
_____
Lunch: _____
_____
Dinner: _____
_____
Snack: _____

SATURDAY
Breakfast: _____
_____
Lunch: _____
_____
Dinner: _____
_____
Snack: _____

SUNDAY
Breakfast: _____
_____
Lunch: _____
_____
Dinner: _____
_____
Snack: _____

SHOPPING LIST:

_____   _____
_____   _____
_____   _____
_____   _____
_____   _____
_____   _____
_____   _____

For the month of: _____

Week of:

MONDAY
Breakfast: _____
_____
Lunch: _____
_____
Dinner: _____
_____
Snack: _____

TUESDAY
Breakfast: _____
_____
Lunch: _____
_____
Dinner: _____
_____
Snack: _____

WEDNESDAY
Breakfast: _____
_____
Lunch: _____
_____
Dinner: _____
_____
Snack: _____

THURSDAY
Breakfast: _____
_____
Lunch: _____
_____
Dinner: _____
_____
Snack: _____

FRIDAY
Breakfast: _____
_____
Lunch: _____
_____
Dinner: _____
_____
Snack: _____

SATURDAY
Breakfast: _____
_____
Lunch: _____
_____
Dinner: _____
_____
Snack: _____

SUNDAY
Breakfast: _____
_____
Lunch: _____
_____
Dinner: _____
_____
Snack: _____

SHOPPING LIST:
_____ _____
_____ _____
_____ _____
_____ _____
_____ _____
_____ _____

For the month of: _____

	MONDAY
Week of:	Breakfast: _____
	Lunch: _____
	Dinner: _____
	Snack: _____

TUESDAY	WEDNESDAY
Breakfast: _____	Breakfast: _____
Lunch: _____	Lunch: _____
Dinner: _____	Dinner: _____
Snack: _____	Snack: _____

THURSDAY	FRIDAY
Breakfast: _____	Breakfast: _____
Lunch: _____	Lunch: _____
Dinner: _____	Dinner: _____
Snack: _____	Snack: _____

SATURDAY	SUNDAY
Breakfast: _____	Breakfast: _____
Lunch: _____	Lunch: _____
Dinner: _____	Dinner: _____
Snack: _____	Snack: _____

SHOPPING LIST:

_____ _____
_____ _____
_____ _____
_____ _____
_____ _____
_____ _____

For the month of: _____

Week of:

MONDAY
Breakfast: _____
Lunch: _____
Dinner: _____
Snack: _____

TUESDAY
Breakfast: _____
Lunch: _____
Dinner: _____
Snack: _____

WEDNESDAY
Breakfast: _____
Lunch: _____
Dinner: _____
Snack: _____

THURSDAY
Breakfast: _____
Lunch: _____
Dinner: _____
Snack: _____

FRIDAY
Breakfast: _____
Lunch: _____
Dinner: _____
Snack: _____

SATURDAY
Breakfast: _____
Lunch: _____
Dinner: _____
Snack: _____

SUNDAY
Breakfast: _____
Lunch: _____
Dinner: _____
Snack: _____

SHOPPING LIST:

For the month of: _____

Week of:	MONDAY
	Breakfast: _____
	Lunch: _____
	Dinner: _____
	Snack: _____

TUESDAY	WEDNESDAY
Breakfast: _____	Breakfast: _____
Lunch: _____	Lunch: _____
Dinner: _____	Dinner: _____
Snack: _____	Snack: _____

THURSDAY	FRIDAY
Breakfast: _____	Breakfast: _____
Lunch: _____	Lunch: _____
Dinner: _____	Dinner: _____
Snack: _____	Snack: _____

SATURDAY	SUNDAY
Breakfast: _____	Breakfast: _____
Lunch: _____	Lunch: _____
Dinner: _____	Dinner: _____
Snack: _____	Snack: _____

SHOPPING LIST:

_____   _____
_____   _____
_____   _____
_____   _____
_____   _____
_____   _____

For the month of: _____

Week of:	MONDAY
	Breakfast: _____
	Lunch: _____
	Dinner: _____
	Snack: _____

TUESDAY	WEDNESDAY
Breakfast: _____	Breakfast: _____
Lunch: _____	Lunch: _____
Dinner: _____	Dinner: _____
Snack: _____	Snack: _____

THURSDAY	FRIDAY
Breakfast: _____	Breakfast: _____
Lunch: _____	Lunch: _____
Dinner: _____	Dinner: _____
Snack: _____	Snack: _____

SATURDAY	SUNDAY
Breakfast: _____	Breakfast: _____
Lunch: _____	Lunch: _____
Dinner: _____	Dinner: _____
Snack: _____	Snack: _____

SHOPPING LIST:

For the month of: _____

Week of: _____

MONDAY
Breakfast: _____

Lunch: _____

Dinner: _____

Snack: _____

TUESDAY
Breakfast: _____

Lunch: _____

Dinner: _____

Snack: _____

WEDNESDAY
Breakfast: _____

Lunch: _____

Dinner: _____

Snack: _____

THURSDAY
Breakfast: _____

Lunch: _____

Dinner: _____

Snack: _____

FRIDAY
Breakfast: _____

Lunch: _____

Dinner: _____

Snack: _____

SATURDAY
Breakfast: _____

Lunch: _____

Dinner: _____

Snack: _____

SUNDAY
Breakfast: _____

Lunch: _____

Dinner: _____

Snack: _____

SHOPPING LIST:
_____

_____

_____

_____

_____

_____

For the month of: _____

Week of:	MONDAY
	Breakfast: _____
	Lunch: _____
	Dinner: _____
	Snack: _____

TUESDAY	WEDNESDAY
Breakfast: _____	Breakfast: _____
Lunch: _____	Lunch: _____
Dinner: _____	Dinner: _____
Snack: _____	Snack: _____

THURSDAY	FRIDAY
Breakfast: _____	Breakfast: _____
Lunch: _____	Lunch: _____
Dinner: _____	Dinner: _____
Snack: _____	Snack: _____

SATURDAY	SUNDAY
Breakfast: _____	Breakfast: _____
Lunch: _____	Lunch: _____
Dinner: _____	Dinner: _____
Snack: _____	Snack: _____

SHOPPING LIST:

For the month of: _____

Week of:	MONDAY
	Breakfast: _____
	Lunch: _____
	Dinner: _____
	Snack: _____

TUESDAY	WEDNESDAY
Breakfast: _____	Breakfast: _____
Lunch: _____	Lunch: _____
Dinner: _____	Dinner: _____
Snack: _____	Snack: _____

THURSDAY	FRIDAY
Breakfast: _____	Breakfast: _____
Lunch: _____	Lunch: _____
Dinner: _____	Dinner: _____
Snack: _____	Snack: _____

SATURDAY	SUNDAY
Breakfast: _____	Breakfast: _____
Lunch: _____	Lunch: _____
Dinner: _____	Dinner: _____
Snack: _____	Snack: _____

SHOPPING LIST:

For the month of: _____

Week of:

MONDAY
Breakfast: _____
Lunch: _____
Dinner: _____
Snack: _____

TUESDAY
Breakfast: _____
Lunch: _____
Dinner: _____
Snack: _____

WEDNESDAY
Breakfast: _____
Lunch: _____
Dinner: _____
Snack: _____

THURSDAY
Breakfast: _____
Lunch: _____
Dinner: _____
Snack: _____

FRIDAY
Breakfast: _____
Lunch: _____
Dinner: _____
Snack: _____

SATURDAY
Breakfast: _____
Lunch: _____
Dinner: _____
Snack: _____

SUNDAY
Breakfast: _____
Lunch: _____
Dinner: _____
Snack: _____

SHOPPING LIST:

_____   _____
_____   _____
_____   _____
_____   _____
_____   _____
_____   _____

For the month of: _____

Week of:	**MONDAY** Breakfast: _____ Lunch: _____ Dinner: _____ Snack: _____
TUESDAY Breakfast: _____ Lunch: _____ Dinner: _____ Snack: _____	**WEDNESDAY** Breakfast: _____ Lunch: _____ Dinner: _____ Snack: _____
THURSDAY Breakfast: _____ Lunch: _____ Dinner: _____ Snack: _____	**FRIDAY** Breakfast: _____ Lunch: _____ Dinner: _____ Snack: _____
SATURDAY Breakfast: _____ Lunch: _____ Dinner: _____ Snack: _____	**SUNDAY** Breakfast: _____ Lunch: _____ Dinner: _____ Snack: _____

SHOPPING LIST:

For the month of: _____

Week of: _____

MONDAY
Breakfast: _____
_____
Lunch: _____
_____
Dinner: _____
_____
Snack: _____

TUESDAY
Breakfast: _____
_____
Lunch: _____
_____
Dinner: _____
_____
Snack: _____

WEDNESDAY
Breakfast: _____
_____
Lunch: _____
_____
Dinner: _____
_____
Snack: _____

THURSDAY
Breakfast: _____
_____
Lunch: _____
_____
Dinner: _____
_____
Snack: _____

FRIDAY
Breakfast: _____
_____
Lunch: _____
_____
Dinner: _____
_____
Snack: _____

SATURDAY
Breakfast: _____
_____
Lunch: _____
_____
Dinner: _____
_____
Snack: _____

SUNDAY
Breakfast: _____
_____
Lunch: _____
_____
Dinner: _____
_____
Snack: _____

SHOPPING LIST:

_____   _____
_____   _____
_____   _____
_____   _____
_____   _____
_____   _____

For the month of: _____

Week of:

MONDAY
Breakfast: _____
_____
Lunch: _____
_____
Dinner: _____
_____
Snack: _____

TUESDAY
Breakfast: _____
_____
Lunch: _____
_____
Dinner: _____
_____
Snack: _____

WEDNESDAY
Breakfast: _____
_____
Lunch: _____
_____
Dinner: _____
_____
Snack: _____

THURSDAY
Breakfast: _____
_____
Lunch: _____
_____
Dinner: _____
_____
Snack: _____

FRIDAY
Breakfast: _____
_____
Lunch: _____
_____
Dinner: _____
_____
Snack: _____

SATURDAY
Breakfast: _____
_____
Lunch: _____
_____
Dinner: _____
_____
Snack: _____

SUNDAY
Breakfast: _____
_____
Lunch: _____
_____
Dinner: _____
_____
Snack: _____

SHOPPING LIST:

_____ _____
_____ _____
_____ _____
_____ _____
_____ _____
_____ _____
_____ _____

For the month of: _____

Week of:

MONDAY
Breakfast: _____
_____
Lunch: _____
_____
Dinner: _____
_____
Snack: _____

TUESDAY
Breakfast: _____
_____
Lunch: _____
_____
Dinner: _____
_____
Snack: _____

WEDNESDAY
Breakfast: _____
_____
Lunch: _____
_____
Dinner: _____
_____
Snack: _____

THURSDAY
Breakfast: _____
_____
Lunch: _____
_____
Dinner: _____
_____
Snack: _____

FRIDAY
Breakfast: _____
_____
Lunch: _____
_____
Dinner: _____
_____
Snack: _____

SATURDAY
Breakfast: _____
_____
Lunch: _____
_____
Dinner: _____
_____
Snack: _____

SUNDAY
Breakfast: _____
_____
Lunch: _____
_____
Dinner: _____
_____
Snack: _____

SHOPPING LIST:

For the month of: _____

Week of:	**MONDAY** Breakfast: _____ Lunch: _____ Dinner: _____ Snack: _____
TUESDAY Breakfast: _____ Lunch: _____ Dinner: _____ Snack: _____	**WEDNESDAY** Breakfast: _____ Lunch: _____ Dinner: _____ Snack: _____
THURSDAY Breakfast: _____ Lunch: _____ Dinner: _____ Snack: _____	**FRIDAY** Breakfast: _____ Lunch: _____ Dinner: _____ Snack: _____
SATURDAY Breakfast: _____ Lunch: _____ Dinner: _____ Snack: _____	**SUNDAY** Breakfast: _____ Lunch: _____ Dinner: _____ Snack: _____

SHOPPING LIST:

For the month of: _____

Week of:	MONDAY
	Breakfast: _____
	Lunch: _____
	Dinner: _____
	Snack: _____

TUESDAY	WEDNESDAY
Breakfast: _____	Breakfast: _____
Lunch: _____	Lunch: _____
Dinner: _____	Dinner: _____
Snack: _____	Snack: _____

THURSDAY	FRIDAY
Breakfast: _____	Breakfast: _____
Lunch: _____	Lunch: _____
Dinner: _____	Dinner: _____
Snack: _____	Snack: _____

SATURDAY	SUNDAY
Breakfast: _____	Breakfast: _____
Lunch: _____	Lunch: _____
Dinner: _____	Dinner: _____
Snack: _____	Snack: _____

SHOPPING LIST:

For the month of: _____

Week of:	**MONDAY** Breakfast: _____ Lunch: _____ Dinner: _____ Snack: _____
TUESDAY Breakfast: _____ Lunch: _____ Dinner: _____ Snack: _____	**WEDNESDAY** Breakfast: _____ Lunch: _____ Dinner: _____ Snack: _____
THURSDAY Breakfast: _____ Lunch: _____ Dinner: _____ Snack: _____	**FRIDAY** Breakfast: _____ Lunch: _____ Dinner: _____ Snack: _____
SATURDAY Breakfast: _____ Lunch: _____ Dinner: _____ Snack: _____	**SUNDAY** Breakfast: _____ Lunch: _____ Dinner: _____ Snack: _____

SHOPPING LIST:

_____   _____
_____   _____
_____   _____
_____   _____
_____   _____
_____   _____
_____   _____

For the month of: _____

Week of:

MONDAY
Breakfast: _____
Lunch: _____
Dinner: _____
Snack: _____

TUESDAY
Breakfast: _____
Lunch: _____
Dinner: _____
Snack: _____

WEDNESDAY
Breakfast: _____
Lunch: _____
Dinner: _____
Snack: _____

THURSDAY
Breakfast: _____
Lunch: _____
Dinner: _____
Snack: _____

FRIDAY
Breakfast: _____
Lunch: _____
Dinner: _____
Snack: _____

SATURDAY
Breakfast: _____
Lunch: _____
Dinner: _____
Snack: _____

SUNDAY
Breakfast: _____
Lunch: _____
Dinner: _____
Snack: _____

SHOPPING LIST:

For the month of: _____

Week of:

MONDAY
Breakfast: _____

Lunch: _____

Dinner: _____

Snack: _____

TUESDAY
Breakfast: _____

Lunch: _____

Dinner: _____

Snack: _____

WEDNESDAY
Breakfast: _____

Lunch: _____

Dinner: _____

Snack: _____

THURSDAY
Breakfast: _____

Lunch: _____

Dinner: _____

Snack: _____

FRIDAY
Breakfast: _____

Lunch: _____

Dinner: _____

Snack: _____

SATURDAY
Breakfast: _____

Lunch: _____

Dinner: _____

Snack: _____

SUNDAY
Breakfast: _____

Lunch: _____

Dinner: _____

Snack: _____

SHOPPING LIST:

_____   _____
_____   _____
_____   _____
_____   _____
_____   _____
_____   _____

For the month of: _____

Week of:

MONDAY
Breakfast: _____
_____
Lunch: _____
_____
Dinner: _____
_____
Snack: _____

TUESDAY
Breakfast: _____
_____
Lunch: _____
_____
Dinner: _____
_____
Snack: _____

WEDNESDAY
Breakfast: _____
_____
Lunch: _____
_____
Dinner: _____
_____
Snack: _____

THURSDAY
Breakfast: _____
_____
Lunch: _____
_____
Dinner: _____
_____
Snack: _____

FRIDAY
Breakfast: _____
_____
Lunch: _____
_____
Dinner: _____
_____
Snack: _____

SATURDAY
Breakfast: _____
_____
Lunch: _____
_____
Dinner: _____
_____
Snack: _____

SUNDAY
Breakfast: _____
_____
Lunch: _____
_____
Dinner: _____
_____
Snack: _____

SHOPPING LIST:

_____   _____
_____   _____
_____   _____
_____   _____
_____   _____
_____   _____

For the month of: _____

	MONDAY
Week of:	Breakfast: _____
	Lunch: _____
	Dinner: _____
	Snack: _____

TUESDAY	WEDNESDAY
Breakfast: _____	Breakfast: _____
Lunch: _____	Lunch: _____
Dinner: _____	Dinner: _____
Snack: _____	Snack: _____

THURSDAY	FRIDAY
Breakfast: _____	Breakfast: _____
Lunch: _____	Lunch: _____
Dinner: _____	Dinner: _____
Snack: _____	Snack: _____

SATURDAY	SUNDAY
Breakfast: _____	Breakfast: _____
Lunch: _____	Lunch: _____
Dinner: _____	Dinner: _____
Snack: _____	Snack: _____

SHOPPING LIST:

For the month of: _____

Week of:

MONDAY
Breakfast: _____

Lunch: _____

Dinner: _____

Snack: _____

TUESDAY
Breakfast: _____

Lunch: _____

Dinner: _____

Snack: _____

WEDNESDAY
Breakfast: _____

Lunch: _____

Dinner: _____

Snack: _____

THURSDAY
Breakfast: _____

Lunch: _____

Dinner: _____

Snack: _____

FRIDAY
Breakfast: _____

Lunch: _____

Dinner: _____

Snack: _____

SATURDAY
Breakfast: _____

Lunch: _____

Dinner: _____

Snack: _____

SUNDAY
Breakfast: _____

Lunch: _____

Dinner: _____

Snack: _____

SHOPPING LIST:

For the month of: _____

Week of:	**MONDAY** Breakfast: _____ Lunch: _____ Dinner: _____ Snack: _____
TUESDAY Breakfast: _____ Lunch: _____ Dinner: _____ Snack: _____	**WEDNESDAY** Breakfast: _____ Lunch: _____ Dinner: _____ Snack: _____
THURSDAY Breakfast: _____ Lunch: _____ Dinner: _____ Snack: _____	**FRIDAY** Breakfast: _____ Lunch: _____ Dinner: _____ Snack: _____
SATURDAY Breakfast: _____ Lunch: _____ Dinner: _____ Snack: _____	**SUNDAY** Breakfast: _____ Lunch: _____ Dinner: _____ Snack: _____

SHOPPING LIST:

_____ _____
_____ _____
_____ _____
_____ _____
_____ _____
_____ _____

For the month of: _____

Week of:

MONDAY
Breakfast: _____
Lunch: _____
Dinner: _____
Snack: _____

TUESDAY
Breakfast: _____
Lunch: _____
Dinner: _____
Snack: _____

WEDNESDAY
Breakfast: _____
Lunch: _____
Dinner: _____
Snack: _____

THURSDAY
Breakfast: _____
Lunch: _____
Dinner: _____
Snack: _____

FRIDAY
Breakfast: _____
Lunch: _____
Dinner: _____
Snack: _____

SATURDAY
Breakfast: _____
Lunch: _____
Dinner: _____
Snack: _____

SUNDAY
Breakfast: _____
Lunch: _____
Dinner: _____
Snack: _____

SHOPPING LIST:

For the month of: _____

Week of:

MONDAY
Breakfast: _____
Lunch: _____
Dinner: _____
Snack: _____

TUESDAY
Breakfast: _____
Lunch: _____
Dinner: _____
Snack: _____

WEDNESDAY
Breakfast: _____
Lunch: _____
Dinner: _____
Snack: _____

THURSDAY
Breakfast: _____
Lunch: _____
Dinner: _____
Snack: _____

FRIDAY
Breakfast: _____
Lunch: _____
Dinner: _____
Snack: _____

SATURDAY
Breakfast: _____
Lunch: _____
Dinner: _____
Snack: _____

SUNDAY
Breakfast: _____
Lunch: _____
Dinner: _____
Snack: _____

SHOPPING LIST:

For the month of: _____

Week of:	**MONDAY** Breakfast: _____ Lunch: _____ Dinner: _____ Snack: _____
TUESDAY Breakfast: _____ Lunch: _____ Dinner: _____ Snack: _____	**WEDNESDAY** Breakfast: _____ Lunch: _____ Dinner: _____ Snack: _____
THURSDAY Breakfast: _____ Lunch: _____ Dinner: _____ Snack: _____	**FRIDAY** Breakfast: _____ Lunch: _____ Dinner: _____ Snack: _____
SATURDAY Breakfast: _____ Lunch: _____ Dinner: _____ Snack: _____	**SUNDAY** Breakfast: _____ Lunch: _____ Dinner: _____ Snack: _____

SHOPPING LIST:

_____   _____
_____   _____
_____   _____
_____   _____
_____   _____
_____   _____

For the month of: _____

Week of:

MONDAY
Breakfast: _____

Lunch: _____

Dinner: _____

Snack: _____

TUESDAY
Breakfast: _____

Lunch: _____

Dinner: _____

Snack: _____

WEDNESDAY
Breakfast: _____

Lunch: _____

Dinner: _____

Snack: _____

THURSDAY
Breakfast: _____

Lunch: _____

Dinner: _____

Snack: _____

FRIDAY
Breakfast: _____

Lunch: _____

Dinner: _____

Snack: _____

SATURDAY
Breakfast: _____

Lunch: _____

Dinner: _____

Snack: _____

SUNDAY
Breakfast: _____

Lunch: _____

Dinner: _____

Snack: _____

SHOPPING LIST:

_____   _____
_____   _____
_____   _____
_____   _____
_____   _____
_____   _____
_____   _____

For the month of: _____

Week of:	MONDAY
	Breakfast: _____
	Lunch: _____
	Dinner: _____
	Snack: _____

TUESDAY	WEDNESDAY
Breakfast: _____	Breakfast: _____
Lunch: _____	Lunch: _____
Dinner: _____	Dinner: _____
Snack: _____	Snack: _____

THURSDAY	FRIDAY
Breakfast: _____	Breakfast: _____
Lunch: _____	Lunch: _____
Dinner: _____	Dinner: _____
Snack: _____	Snack: _____

SATURDAY	SUNDAY
Breakfast: _____	Breakfast: _____
Lunch: _____	Lunch: _____
Dinner: _____	Dinner: _____
Snack: _____	Snack: _____

SHOPPING LIST:

_____   _____
_____   _____
_____   _____
_____   _____
_____   _____
_____   _____

For the month of: _____

Week of:	MONDAY
	Breakfast: _____
	Lunch: _____
	Dinner: _____
	Snack: _____

TUESDAY	WEDNESDAY
Breakfast: _____	Breakfast: _____
Lunch: _____	Lunch: _____
Dinner: _____	Dinner: _____
Snack: _____	Snack: _____

THURSDAY	FRIDAY
Breakfast: _____	Breakfast: _____
Lunch: _____	Lunch: _____
Dinner: _____	Dinner: _____
Snack: _____	Snack: _____

SATURDAY	SUNDAY
Breakfast: _____	Breakfast: _____
Lunch: _____	Lunch: _____
Dinner: _____	Dinner: _____
Snack: _____	Snack: _____

SHOPPING LIST:

For the month of: _____

	MONDAY
Week of:	Breakfast: _____
	Lunch: _____
	Dinner: _____
	Snack: _____

TUESDAY	WEDNESDAY
Breakfast: _____	Breakfast: _____
Lunch: _____	Lunch: _____
Dinner: _____	Dinner: _____
Snack: _____	Snack: _____

THURSDAY	FRIDAY
Breakfast: _____	Breakfast: _____
Lunch: _____	Lunch: _____
Dinner: _____	Dinner: _____
Snack: _____	Snack: _____

SATURDAY	SUNDAY
Breakfast: _____	Breakfast: _____
Lunch: _____	Lunch: _____
Dinner: _____	Dinner: _____
Snack: _____	Snack: _____

SHOPPING LIST:

_____   _____
_____   _____
_____   _____
_____   _____
_____   _____
_____   _____

For the month of: _____

Week of:

MONDAY
Breakfast: _____

Lunch: _____

Dinner: _____

Snack: _____

TUESDAY
Breakfast: _____

Lunch: _____

Dinner: _____

Snack: _____

WEDNESDAY
Breakfast: _____

Lunch: _____

Dinner: _____

Snack: _____

THURSDAY
Breakfast: _____

Lunch: _____

Dinner: _____

Snack: _____

FRIDAY
Breakfast: _____

Lunch: _____

Dinner: _____

Snack: _____

SATURDAY
Breakfast: _____

Lunch: _____

Dinner: _____

Snack: _____

SUNDAY
Breakfast: _____

Lunch: _____

Dinner: _____

Snack: _____

SHOPPING LIST:

For the month of: _____

Week of:

MONDAY
Breakfast: _____
_____
Lunch: _____
_____
Dinner: _____
_____
Snack: _____

TUESDAY
Breakfast: _____
_____
Lunch: _____
_____
Dinner: _____
_____
Snack: _____

WEDNESDAY
Breakfast: _____
_____
Lunch: _____
_____
Dinner: _____
_____
Snack: _____

THURSDAY
Breakfast: _____
_____
Lunch: _____
_____
Dinner: _____
_____
Snack: _____

FRIDAY
Breakfast: _____
_____
Lunch: _____
_____
Dinner: _____
_____
Snack: _____

SATURDAY
Breakfast: _____
_____
Lunch: _____
_____
Dinner: _____
_____
Snack: _____

SUNDAY
Breakfast: _____
_____
Lunch: _____
_____
Dinner: _____
_____
Snack: _____

SHOPPING LIST:
_____ _____
_____ _____
_____ _____
_____ _____
_____ _____
_____ _____

For the month of: _____

Week of:

MONDAY
Breakfast: _____
_____
Lunch: _____
_____
Dinner: _____
_____
Snack: _____

TUESDAY
Breakfast: _____
_____
Lunch: _____
_____
Dinner: _____
_____
Snack: _____

WEDNESDAY
Breakfast: _____
_____
Lunch: _____
_____
Dinner: _____
_____
Snack: _____

THURSDAY
Breakfast: _____
_____
Lunch: _____
_____
Dinner: _____
_____
Snack: _____

FRIDAY
Breakfast: _____
_____
Lunch: _____
_____
Dinner: _____
_____
Snack: _____

SATURDAY
Breakfast: _____
_____
Lunch: _____
_____
Dinner: _____
_____
Snack: _____

SUNDAY
Breakfast: _____
_____
Lunch: _____
_____
Dinner: _____
_____
Snack: _____

SHOPPING LIST:

_____ _____
_____ _____
_____ _____
_____ _____
_____ _____
_____ _____

For the month of: _____

Week of:	**MONDAY** Breakfast: _____ Lunch: _____ Dinner: _____ Snack: _____
TUESDAY Breakfast: _____ Lunch: _____ Dinner: _____ Snack: _____	**WEDNESDAY** Breakfast: _____ Lunch: _____ Dinner: _____ Snack: _____
THURSDAY Breakfast: _____ Lunch: _____ Dinner: _____ Snack: _____	**FRIDAY** Breakfast: _____ Lunch: _____ Dinner: _____ Snack: _____
SATURDAY Breakfast: _____ Lunch: _____ Dinner: _____ Snack: _____	**SUNDAY** Breakfast: _____ Lunch: _____ Dinner: _____ Snack: _____

SHOPPING LIST:

For the month of: _____

Week of:

MONDAY
Breakfast: _____
Lunch: _____
Dinner: _____
Snack: _____

TUESDAY
Breakfast: _____
Lunch: _____
Dinner: _____
Snack: _____

WEDNESDAY
Breakfast: _____
Lunch: _____
Dinner: _____
Snack: _____

THURSDAY
Breakfast: _____
Lunch: _____
Dinner: _____
Snack: _____

FRIDAY
Breakfast: _____
Lunch: _____
Dinner: _____
Snack: _____

SATURDAY
Breakfast: _____
Lunch: _____
Dinner: _____
Snack: _____

SUNDAY
Breakfast: _____
Lunch: _____
Dinner: _____
Snack: _____

SHOPPING LIST:

For the month of: _____

Week of:

MONDAY
Breakfast: _____
_____
Lunch: _____
_____
Dinner: _____
_____
Snack: _____

TUESDAY
Breakfast: _____
_____
Lunch: _____
_____
Dinner: _____
_____
Snack: _____

WEDNESDAY
Breakfast: _____
_____
Lunch: _____
_____
Dinner: _____
_____
Snack: _____

THURSDAY
Breakfast: _____
_____
Lunch: _____
_____
Dinner: _____
_____
Snack: _____

FRIDAY
Breakfast: _____
_____
Lunch: _____
_____
Dinner: _____
_____
Snack: _____

SATURDAY
Breakfast: _____
_____
Lunch: _____
_____
Dinner: _____
_____
Snack: _____

SUNDAY
Breakfast: _____
_____
Lunch: _____
_____
Dinner: _____
_____
Snack: _____

SHOPPING LIST:

For the month of: _____

Week of:

MONDAY
Breakfast: _____
Lunch: _____
Dinner: _____
Snack: _____

TUESDAY
Breakfast: _____
Lunch: _____
Dinner: _____
Snack: _____

WEDNESDAY
Breakfast: _____
Lunch: _____
Dinner: _____
Snack: _____

THURSDAY
Breakfast: _____
Lunch: _____
Dinner: _____
Snack: _____

FRIDAY
Breakfast: _____
Lunch: _____
Dinner: _____
Snack: _____

SATURDAY
Breakfast: _____
Lunch: _____
Dinner: _____
Snack: _____

SUNDAY
Breakfast: _____
Lunch: _____
Dinner: _____
Snack: _____

SHOPPING LIST:

For the month of: _____

Week of:

MONDAY
Breakfast: _____
_____
Lunch: _____
_____
Dinner: _____
_____
Snack: _____

TUESDAY
Breakfast: _____
_____
Lunch: _____
_____
Dinner: _____
_____
Snack: _____

WEDNESDAY
Breakfast: _____
_____
Lunch: _____
_____
Dinner: _____
_____
Snack: _____

THURSDAY
Breakfast: _____
_____
Lunch: _____
_____
Dinner: _____
_____
Snack: _____

FRIDAY
Breakfast: _____
_____
Lunch: _____
_____
Dinner: _____
_____
Snack: _____

SATURDAY
Breakfast: _____
_____
Lunch: _____
_____
Dinner: _____
_____
Snack: _____

SUNDAY
Breakfast: _____
_____
Lunch: _____
_____
Dinner: _____
_____
Snack: _____

SHOPPING LIST:

_____ _____
_____ _____
_____ _____
_____ _____
_____ _____
_____ _____

For the month of: _____

Week of:

MONDAY
Breakfast: _____
Lunch: _____
Dinner: _____
Snack: _____

TUESDAY
Breakfast: _____
Lunch: _____
Dinner: _____
Snack: _____

WEDNESDAY
Breakfast: _____
Lunch: _____
Dinner: _____
Snack: _____

THURSDAY
Breakfast: _____
Lunch: _____
Dinner: _____
Snack: _____

FRIDAY
Breakfast: _____
Lunch: _____
Dinner: _____
Snack: _____

SATURDAY
Breakfast: _____
Lunch: _____
Dinner: _____
Snack: _____

SUNDAY
Breakfast: _____
Lunch: _____
Dinner: _____
Snack: _____

SHOPPING LIST:

For the month of: _____

Week of:	**MONDAY**
	Breakfast: _____
	Lunch: _____
	Dinner: _____
	Snack: _____

TUESDAY	**WEDNESDAY**
Breakfast: _____	Breakfast: _____
Lunch: _____	Lunch: _____
Dinner: _____	Dinner: _____
Snack: _____	Snack: _____

THURSDAY	**FRIDAY**
Breakfast: _____	Breakfast: _____
Lunch: _____	Lunch: _____
Dinner: _____	Dinner: _____
Snack: _____	Snack: _____

SATURDAY	**SUNDAY**
Breakfast: _____	Breakfast: _____
Lunch: _____	Lunch: _____
Dinner: _____	Dinner: _____
Snack: _____	Snack: _____

SHOPPING LIST:

_____ _____
_____ _____
_____ _____
_____ _____
_____ _____
_____ _____

For the month of: _____

Week of:	MONDAY
	Breakfast: _____
	Lunch: _____
	Dinner: _____
	Snack: _____

TUESDAY	WEDNESDAY
Breakfast: _____	Breakfast: _____
Lunch: _____	Lunch: _____
Dinner: _____	Dinner: _____
Snack: _____	Snack: _____

THURSDAY	FRIDAY
Breakfast: _____	Breakfast: _____
Lunch: _____	Lunch: _____
Dinner: _____	Dinner: _____
Snack: _____	Snack: _____

SATURDAY	SUNDAY
Breakfast: _____	Breakfast: _____
Lunch: _____	Lunch: _____
Dinner: _____	Dinner: _____
Snack: _____	Snack: _____

SHOPPING LIST:

_____   _____
_____   _____
_____   _____
_____   _____
_____   _____
_____   _____
_____   _____

For the month of: _____

Week of:	**MONDAY** Breakfast: _____ Lunch: _____ Dinner: _____ Snack: _____

TUESDAY	**WEDNESDAY**
Breakfast: _____	Breakfast: _____
Lunch: _____	Lunch: _____
Dinner: _____	Dinner: _____
Snack: _____	Snack: _____

THURSDAY	**FRIDAY**
Breakfast: _____	Breakfast: _____
Lunch: _____	Lunch: _____
Dinner: _____	Dinner: _____
Snack: _____	Snack: _____

SATURDAY	**SUNDAY**
Breakfast: _____	Breakfast: _____
Lunch: _____	Lunch: _____
Dinner: _____	Dinner: _____
Snack: _____	Snack: _____

SHOPPING LIST:

_____ _____
_____ _____
_____ _____
_____ _____
_____ _____
_____ _____

For the month of: _____

Week of:	MONDAY
	Breakfast: _____
	Lunch: _____
	Dinner: _____
	Snack: _____

TUESDAY	WEDNESDAY
Breakfast: _____	Breakfast: _____
Lunch: _____	Lunch: _____
Dinner: _____	Dinner: _____
Snack: _____	Snack: _____

THURSDAY	FRIDAY
Breakfast: _____	Breakfast: _____
Lunch: _____	Lunch: _____
Dinner: _____	Dinner: _____
Snack: _____	Snack: _____

SATURDAY	SUNDAY
Breakfast: _____	Breakfast: _____
Lunch: _____	Lunch: _____
Dinner: _____	Dinner: _____
Snack: _____	Snack: _____

SHOPPING LIST:

For the month of: _____

Week of:	**MONDAY**
	Breakfast: _____
	Lunch: _____
	Dinner: _____
	Snack: _____

TUESDAY	**WEDNESDAY**
Breakfast: _____	Breakfast: _____
Lunch: _____	Lunch: _____
Dinner: _____	Dinner: _____
Snack: _____	Snack: _____

THURSDAY	**FRIDAY**
Breakfast: _____	Breakfast: _____
Lunch: _____	Lunch: _____
Dinner: _____	Dinner: _____
Snack: _____	Snack: _____

SATURDAY	**SUNDAY**
Breakfast: _____	Breakfast: _____
Lunch: _____	Lunch: _____
Dinner: _____	Dinner: _____
Snack: _____	Snack: _____

SHOPPING LIST:

For the month of: _____

Week of:

MONDAY
Breakfast: _____
_____
Lunch: _____
_____
Dinner: _____
_____
Snack: _____

TUESDAY
Breakfast: _____
_____
Lunch: _____
_____
Dinner: _____
_____
Snack: _____

WEDNESDAY
Breakfast: _____
_____
Lunch: _____
_____
Dinner: _____
_____
Snack: _____

THURSDAY
Breakfast: _____
_____
Lunch: _____
_____
Dinner: _____
_____
Snack: _____

FRIDAY
Breakfast: _____
_____
Lunch: _____
_____
Dinner: _____
_____
Snack: _____

SATURDAY
Breakfast: _____
_____
Lunch: _____
_____
Dinner: _____
_____
Snack: _____

SUNDAY
Breakfast: _____
_____
Lunch: _____
_____
Dinner: _____
_____
Snack: _____

SHOPPING LIST:

_____   _____
_____   _____
_____   _____
_____   _____
_____   _____
_____   _____
_____   _____

For the month of: _____

Week of:

MONDAY
Breakfast: _____
Lunch: _____
Dinner: _____
Snack: _____

TUESDAY
Breakfast: _____
Lunch: _____
Dinner: _____
Snack: _____

WEDNESDAY
Breakfast: _____
Lunch: _____
Dinner: _____
Snack: _____

THURSDAY
Breakfast: _____
Lunch: _____
Dinner: _____
Snack: _____

FRIDAY
Breakfast: _____
Lunch: _____
Dinner: _____
Snack: _____

SATURDAY
Breakfast: _____
Lunch: _____
Dinner: _____
Snack: _____

SUNDAY
Breakfast: _____
Lunch: _____
Dinner: _____
Snack: _____

SHOPPING LIST:

_____   _____
_____   _____
_____   _____
_____   _____
_____   _____
_____   _____

For the month of: _____

Week of:

MONDAY
Breakfast: _____

Lunch: _____

Dinner: _____

Snack: _____

TUESDAY
Breakfast: _____

Lunch: _____

Dinner: _____

Snack: _____

WEDNESDAY
Breakfast: _____

Lunch: _____

Dinner: _____

Snack: _____

THURSDAY
Breakfast: _____

Lunch: _____

Dinner: _____

Snack: _____

FRIDAY
Breakfast: _____

Lunch: _____

Dinner: _____

Snack: _____

SATURDAY
Breakfast: _____

Lunch: _____

Dinner: _____

Snack: _____

SUNDAY
Breakfast: _____

Lunch: _____

Dinner: _____

Snack: _____

SHOPPING LIST:

_____ _____
_____ _____
_____ _____
_____ _____
_____ _____
_____ _____

For the month of: _____

	MONDAY
Week of:	Breakfast: _____
━━━❦❧━━━	Lunch: _____
	Dinner: _____
	Snack: _____

TUESDAY	WEDNESDAY
Breakfast: _____	Breakfast: _____
Lunch: _____	Lunch: _____
Dinner: _____	Dinner: _____
Snack: _____	Snack: _____

THURSDAY	FRIDAY
Breakfast: _____	Breakfast: _____
Lunch: _____	Lunch: _____
Dinner: _____	Dinner: _____
Snack: _____	Snack: _____

SATURDAY	SUNDAY
Breakfast: _____	Breakfast: _____
Lunch: _____	Lunch: _____
Dinner: _____	Dinner: _____
Snack: _____	Snack: _____

SHOPPING LIST:

_____   _____
_____   _____
_____   _____
_____   _____
_____   _____
_____   _____

For the month of: _____

Week of:	MONDAY
	Breakfast: _____
	Lunch: _____
	Dinner: _____
	Snack: _____

TUESDAY	WEDNESDAY
Breakfast: _____	Breakfast: _____
Lunch: _____	Lunch: _____
Dinner: _____	Dinner: _____
Snack: _____	Snack: _____

THURSDAY	FRIDAY
Breakfast: _____	Breakfast: _____
Lunch: _____	Lunch: _____
Dinner: _____	Dinner: _____
Snack: _____	Snack: _____

SATURDAY	SUNDAY
Breakfast: _____	Breakfast: _____
Lunch: _____	Lunch: _____
Dinner: _____	Dinner: _____
Snack: _____	Snack: _____

SHOPPING LIST:

_____   _____
_____   _____
_____   _____
_____   _____
_____   _____
_____   _____

For the month of: _____

Week of:

MONDAY
Breakfast: _____
Lunch: _____
Dinner: _____
Snack: _____

TUESDAY
Breakfast: _____
Lunch: _____
Dinner: _____
Snack: _____

WEDNESDAY
Breakfast: _____
Lunch: _____
Dinner: _____
Snack: _____

THURSDAY
Breakfast: _____
Lunch: _____
Dinner: _____
Snack: _____

FRIDAY
Breakfast: _____
Lunch: _____
Dinner: _____
Snack: _____

SATURDAY
Breakfast: _____
Lunch: _____
Dinner: _____
Snack: _____

SUNDAY
Breakfast: _____
Lunch: _____
Dinner: _____
Snack: _____

SHOPPING LIST:

For the month of: _____

Week of:

MONDAY
Breakfast: _____
Lunch: _____
Dinner: _____
Snack: _____

TUESDAY
Breakfast: _____
Lunch: _____
Dinner: _____
Snack: _____

WEDNESDAY
Breakfast: _____
Lunch: _____
Dinner: _____
Snack: _____

THURSDAY
Breakfast: _____
Lunch: _____
Dinner: _____
Snack: _____

FRIDAY
Breakfast: _____
Lunch: _____
Dinner: _____
Snack: _____

SATURDAY
Breakfast: _____
Lunch: _____
Dinner: _____
Snack: _____

SUNDAY
Breakfast: _____
Lunch: _____
Dinner: _____
Snack: _____

SHOPPING LIST:

_____   _____
_____   _____
_____   _____
_____   _____
_____   _____
_____   _____
_____   _____

For the month of: _____

Week of:	**MONDAY**
	Breakfast: _____
	Lunch: _____
	Dinner: _____
	Snack: _____

TUESDAY	**WEDNESDAY**
Breakfast: _____	Breakfast: _____
Lunch: _____	Lunch: _____
Dinner: _____	Dinner: _____
Snack: _____	Snack: _____

THURSDAY	**FRIDAY**
Breakfast: _____	Breakfast: _____
Lunch: _____	Lunch: _____
Dinner: _____	Dinner: _____
Snack: _____	Snack: _____

SATURDAY	**SUNDAY**
Breakfast: _____	Breakfast: _____
Lunch: _____	Lunch: _____
Dinner: _____	Dinner: _____
Snack: _____	Snack: _____

SHOPPING LIST:

_____   _____
_____   _____
_____   _____
_____   _____
_____   _____
_____   _____

For the month of: _____

Week of:

MONDAY

Breakfast: _____

Lunch: _____

Dinner: _____

Snack: _____

TUESDAY

Breakfast: _____

Lunch: _____

Dinner: _____

Snack: _____

WEDNESDAY

Breakfast: _____

Lunch: _____

Dinner: _____

Snack: _____

THURSDAY

Breakfast: _____

Lunch: _____

Dinner: _____

Snack: _____

FRIDAY

Breakfast: _____

Lunch: _____

Dinner: _____

Snack: _____

SATURDAY

Breakfast: _____

Lunch: _____

Dinner: _____

Snack: _____

SUNDAY

Breakfast: _____

Lunch: _____

Dinner: _____

Snack: _____

SHOPPING LIST:

For the month of: _____

Week of:	MONDAY
	Breakfast: _____
	Lunch: _____
	Dinner: _____
	Snack: _____

TUESDAY	WEDNESDAY
Breakfast: _____	Breakfast: _____
Lunch: _____	Lunch: _____
Dinner: _____	Dinner: _____
Snack: _____	Snack: _____

THURSDAY	FRIDAY
Breakfast: _____	Breakfast: _____
Lunch: _____	Lunch: _____
Dinner: _____	Dinner: _____
Snack: _____	Snack: _____

SATURDAY	SUNDAY
Breakfast: _____	Breakfast: _____
Lunch: _____	Lunch: _____
Dinner: _____	Dinner: _____
Snack: _____	Snack: _____

SHOPPING LIST:

_____ _____
_____ _____
_____ _____
_____ _____
_____ _____
_____ _____
_____ _____

For the month of: _____

Week of:

MONDAY
Breakfast: _____
_____
Lunch: _____
_____
Dinner: _____
_____
Snack: _____

TUESDAY
Breakfast: _____
Lunch: _____
Dinner: _____
Snack: _____

WEDNESDAY
Breakfast: _____
Lunch: _____
Dinner: _____
Snack: _____

THURSDAY
Breakfast: _____
Lunch: _____
Dinner: _____
Snack: _____

FRIDAY
Breakfast: _____
Lunch: _____
Dinner: _____
Snack: _____

SATURDAY
Breakfast: _____
Lunch: _____
Dinner: _____
Snack: _____

SUNDAY
Breakfast: _____
Lunch: _____
Dinner: _____
Snack: _____

SHOPPING LIST:

_____ _____
_____ _____
_____ _____
_____ _____
_____ _____
_____ _____
_____ _____

For the month of: _____

Week of:

MONDAY
Breakfast: _____
Lunch: _____
Dinner: _____
Snack: _____

TUESDAY
Breakfast: _____
Lunch: _____
Dinner: _____
Snack: _____

WEDNESDAY
Breakfast: _____
Lunch: _____
Dinner: _____
Snack: _____

THURSDAY
Breakfast: _____
Lunch: _____
Dinner: _____
Snack: _____

FRIDAY
Breakfast: _____
Lunch: _____
Dinner: _____
Snack: _____

SATURDAY
Breakfast: _____
Lunch: _____
Dinner: _____
Snack: _____

SUNDAY
Breakfast: _____
Lunch: _____
Dinner: _____
Snack: _____

SHOPPING LIST:

For the month of: _____

Week of:

MONDAY
Breakfast: _____

Lunch: _____

Dinner: _____

Snack: _____

TUESDAY
Breakfast: _____

Lunch: _____

Dinner: _____

Snack: _____

WEDNESDAY
Breakfast: _____

Lunch: _____

Dinner: _____

Snack: _____

THURSDAY
Breakfast: _____

Lunch: _____

Dinner: _____

Snack: _____

FRIDAY
Breakfast: _____

Lunch: _____

Dinner: _____

Snack: _____

SATURDAY
Breakfast: _____

Lunch: _____

Dinner: _____

Snack: _____

SUNDAY
Breakfast: _____

Lunch: _____

Dinner: _____

Snack: _____

SHOPPING LIST:

_____   _____
_____   _____
_____   _____
_____   _____
_____   _____
_____   _____

For the month of: _____

Week of:	**MONDAY**
	Breakfast: _____
	Lunch: _____
	Dinner: _____
	Snack: _____

TUESDAY	**WEDNESDAY**
Breakfast: _____	Breakfast: _____
Lunch: _____	Lunch: _____
Dinner: _____	Dinner: _____
Snack: _____	Snack: _____

THURSDAY	**FRIDAY**
Breakfast: _____	Breakfast: _____
Lunch: _____	Lunch: _____
Dinner: _____	Dinner: _____
Snack: _____	Snack: _____

SATURDAY	**SUNDAY**
Breakfast: _____	Breakfast: _____
Lunch: _____	Lunch: _____
Dinner: _____	Dinner: _____
Snack: _____	Snack: _____

SHOPPING LIST:

_____ _____
_____ _____
_____ _____
_____ _____
_____ _____
_____ _____

For the month of: _____

Week of:	**MONDAY** Breakfast: _____ Lunch: _____ Dinner: _____ Snack: _____
TUESDAY Breakfast: _____ Lunch: _____ Dinner: _____ Snack: _____	**WEDNESDAY** Breakfast: _____ Lunch: _____ Dinner: _____ Snack: _____
THURSDAY Breakfast: _____ Lunch: _____ Dinner: _____ Snack: _____	**FRIDAY** Breakfast: _____ Lunch: _____ Dinner: _____ Snack: _____
SATURDAY Breakfast: _____ Lunch: _____ Dinner: _____ Snack: _____	**SUNDAY** Breakfast: _____ Lunch: _____ Dinner: _____ Snack: _____

SHOPPING LIST:

_____   _____
_____   _____
_____   _____
_____   _____
_____   _____
_____   _____

For the month of: _____

Week of:	**MONDAY**
	Breakfast: _____
	Lunch: _____
	Dinner: _____
	Snack: _____

TUESDAY	**WEDNESDAY**
Breakfast: _____	Breakfast: _____
Lunch: _____	Lunch: _____
Dinner: _____	Dinner: _____
Snack: _____	Snack: _____

THURSDAY	**FRIDAY**
Breakfast: _____	Breakfast: _____
Lunch: _____	Lunch: _____
Dinner: _____	Dinner: _____
Snack: _____	Snack: _____

SATURDAY	**SUNDAY**
Breakfast: _____	Breakfast: _____
Lunch: _____	Lunch: _____
Dinner: _____	Dinner: _____
Snack: _____	Snack: _____

SHOPPING LIST:

For the month of: _____

Week of:	**MONDAY**
	Breakfast: _____
	Lunch: _____
	Dinner: _____
	Snack: _____

TUESDAY	**WEDNESDAY**
Breakfast: _____	Breakfast: _____
Lunch: _____	Lunch: _____
Dinner: _____	Dinner: _____
Snack: _____	Snack: _____

THURSDAY	**FRIDAY**
Breakfast: _____	Breakfast: _____
Lunch: _____	Lunch: _____
Dinner: _____	Dinner: _____
Snack: _____	Snack: _____

SATURDAY	**SUNDAY**
Breakfast: _____	Breakfast: _____
Lunch: _____	Lunch: _____
Dinner: _____	Dinner: _____
Snack: _____	Snack: _____

SHOPPING LIST:

_____ _____
_____ _____
_____ _____
_____ _____
_____ _____
_____ _____

For the month of: _____

Week of:

MONDAY
Breakfast: _____
_____
Lunch: _____
_____
Dinner: _____
_____
Snack: _____

TUESDAY
Breakfast: _____
_____
Lunch: _____
_____
Dinner: _____
_____
Snack: _____

WEDNESDAY
Breakfast: _____
_____
Lunch: _____
_____
Dinner: _____
_____
Snack: _____

THURSDAY
Breakfast: _____
_____
Lunch: _____
_____
Dinner: _____
_____
Snack: _____

FRIDAY
Breakfast: _____
_____
Lunch: _____
_____
Dinner: _____
_____
Snack: _____

SATURDAY
Breakfast: _____
_____
Lunch: _____
_____
Dinner: _____
_____
Snack: _____

SUNDAY
Breakfast: _____
_____
Lunch: _____
_____
Dinner: _____
_____
Snack: _____

SHOPPING LIST:

For the month of: _____

Week of:

MONDAY
Breakfast: _____

Lunch: _____

Dinner: _____

Snack: _____

TUESDAY
Breakfast: _____

Lunch: _____

Dinner: _____

Snack: _____

WEDNESDAY
Breakfast: _____

Lunch: _____

Dinner: _____

Snack: _____

THURSDAY
Breakfast: _____

Lunch: _____

Dinner: _____

Snack: _____

FRIDAY
Breakfast: _____

Lunch: _____

Dinner: _____

Snack: _____

SATURDAY
Breakfast: _____

Lunch: _____

Dinner: _____

Snack: _____

SUNDAY
Breakfast: _____

Lunch: _____

Dinner: _____

Snack: _____

SHOPPING LIST:

For the month of: _____

Week of:

MONDAY
Breakfast: _____
Lunch: _____
Dinner: _____
Snack: _____

TUESDAY
Breakfast: _____
Lunch: _____
Dinner: _____
Snack: _____

WEDNESDAY
Breakfast: _____
Lunch: _____
Dinner: _____
Snack: _____

THURSDAY
Breakfast: _____
Lunch: _____
Dinner: _____
Snack: _____

FRIDAY
Breakfast: _____
Lunch: _____
Dinner: _____
Snack: _____

SATURDAY
Breakfast: _____
Lunch: _____
Dinner: _____
Snack: _____

SUNDAY
Breakfast: _____
Lunch: _____
Dinner: _____
Snack: _____

SHOPPING LIST:

For the month of: _____

Week of:	**MONDAY** Breakfast: _____ Lunch: _____ Dinner: _____ Snack: _____
TUESDAY Breakfast: _____ Lunch: _____ Dinner: _____ Snack: _____	**WEDNESDAY** Breakfast: _____ Lunch: _____ Dinner: _____ Snack: _____
THURSDAY Breakfast: _____ Lunch: _____ Dinner: _____ Snack: _____	**FRIDAY** Breakfast: _____ Lunch: _____ Dinner: _____ Snack: _____
SATURDAY Breakfast: _____ Lunch: _____ Dinner: _____ Snack: _____	**SUNDAY** Breakfast: _____ Lunch: _____ Dinner: _____ Snack: _____

SHOPPING LIST:

For the month of: _____

Week of:

MONDAY
Breakfast: _____

Lunch: _____

Dinner: _____

Snack: _____

TUESDAY
Breakfast: _____

Lunch: _____

Dinner: _____

Snack: _____

WEDNESDAY
Breakfast: _____

Lunch: _____

Dinner: _____

Snack: _____

THURSDAY
Breakfast: _____

Lunch: _____

Dinner: _____

Snack: _____

FRIDAY
Breakfast: _____

Lunch: _____

Dinner: _____

Snack: _____

SATURDAY
Breakfast: _____

Lunch: _____

Dinner: _____

Snack: _____

SUNDAY
Breakfast: _____

Lunch: _____

Dinner: _____

Snack: _____

SHOPPING LIST:

For the month of: _____

Week of:	**MONDAY** Breakfast: _____ Lunch: _____ Dinner: _____ Snack: _____

TUESDAY Breakfast: _____ Lunch: _____ Dinner: _____ Snack: _____	**WEDNESDAY** Breakfast: _____ Lunch: _____ Dinner: _____ Snack: _____
THURSDAY Breakfast: _____ Lunch: _____ Dinner: _____ Snack: _____	**FRIDAY** Breakfast: _____ Lunch: _____ Dinner: _____ Snack: _____
SATURDAY Breakfast: _____ Lunch: _____ Dinner: _____ Snack: _____	**SUNDAY** Breakfast: _____ Lunch: _____ Dinner: _____ Snack: _____

SHOPPING LIST:

_____ _____
_____ _____
_____ _____
_____ _____
_____ _____
_____ _____

For the month of: _____

Week of:

MONDAY
Breakfast: _____

Lunch: _____

Dinner: _____

Snack: _____

TUESDAY
Breakfast: _____

Lunch: _____

Dinner: _____

Snack: _____

WEDNESDAY
Breakfast: _____

Lunch: _____

Dinner: _____

Snack: _____

THURSDAY
Breakfast: _____

Lunch: _____

Dinner: _____

Snack: _____

FRIDAY
Breakfast: _____

Lunch: _____

Dinner: _____

Snack: _____

SATURDAY
Breakfast: _____

Lunch: _____

Dinner: _____

Snack: _____

SUNDAY
Breakfast: _____

Lunch: _____

Dinner: _____

Snack: _____

SHOPPING LIST:

_____   _____
_____   _____
_____   _____
_____   _____
_____   _____
_____   _____
_____   _____

For the month of: _____

Week of:	MONDAY
	Breakfast: _____
	Lunch: _____
	Dinner: _____
	Snack: _____

TUESDAY	WEDNESDAY
Breakfast: _____	Breakfast: _____
Lunch: _____	Lunch: _____
Dinner: _____	Dinner: _____
Snack: _____	Snack: _____

THURSDAY	FRIDAY
Breakfast: _____	Breakfast: _____
Lunch: _____	Lunch: _____
Dinner: _____	Dinner: _____
Snack: _____	Snack: _____

SATURDAY	SUNDAY
Breakfast: _____	Breakfast: _____
Lunch: _____	Lunch: _____
Dinner: _____	Dinner: _____
Snack: _____	Snack: _____

SHOPPING LIST:

_____ _____
_____ _____
_____ _____
_____ _____
_____ _____
_____ _____
_____ _____

For the month of: _____

Week of:

MONDAY
Breakfast: _____
Lunch: _____
Dinner: _____
Snack: _____

TUESDAY
Breakfast: _____
Lunch: _____
Dinner: _____
Snack: _____

WEDNESDAY
Breakfast: _____
Lunch: _____
Dinner: _____
Snack: _____

THURSDAY
Breakfast: _____
Lunch: _____
Dinner: _____
Snack: _____

FRIDAY
Breakfast: _____
Lunch: _____
Dinner: _____
Snack: _____

SATURDAY
Breakfast: _____
Lunch: _____
Dinner: _____
Snack: _____

SUNDAY
Breakfast: _____
Lunch: _____
Dinner: _____
Snack: _____

SHOPPING LIST:

_____ _____
_____ _____
_____ _____
_____ _____
_____ _____
_____ _____

For the month of: _____

Week of:

MONDAY
Breakfast: _____

Lunch: _____

Dinner: _____

Snack: _____

TUESDAY
Breakfast: _____

Lunch: _____

Dinner: _____

Snack: _____

WEDNESDAY
Breakfast: _____

Lunch: _____

Dinner: _____

Snack: _____

THURSDAY
Breakfast: _____

Lunch: _____

Dinner: _____

Snack: _____

FRIDAY
Breakfast: _____

Lunch: _____

Dinner: _____

Snack: _____

SATURDAY
Breakfast: _____

Lunch: _____

Dinner: _____

Snack: _____

SUNDAY
Breakfast: _____

Lunch: _____

Dinner: _____

Snack: _____

SHOPPING LIST:

For the month of: _____

Week of: _____	MONDAY Breakfast: _____ Lunch: _____ Dinner: _____ Snack: _____
TUESDAY Breakfast: _____ Lunch: _____ Dinner: _____ Snack: _____	WEDNESDAY Breakfast: _____ Lunch: _____ Dinner: _____ Snack: _____
THURSDAY Breakfast: _____ Lunch: _____ Dinner: _____ Snack: _____	FRIDAY Breakfast: _____ Lunch: _____ Dinner: _____ Snack: _____
SATURDAY Breakfast: _____ Lunch: _____ Dinner: _____ Snack: _____	SUNDAY Breakfast: _____ Lunch: _____ Dinner: _____ Snack: _____

SHOPPING LIST:

_____ _____
_____ _____
_____ _____
_____ _____
_____ _____
_____ _____
_____ _____

For the month of: _____

Week of:	**MONDAY** Breakfast: _____ Lunch: _____ Dinner: _____ Snack: _____
TUESDAY Breakfast: _____ Lunch: _____ Dinner: _____ Snack: _____	**WEDNESDAY** Breakfast: _____ Lunch: _____ Dinner: _____ Snack: _____
THURSDAY Breakfast: _____ Lunch: _____ Dinner: _____ Snack: _____	**FRIDAY** Breakfast: _____ Lunch: _____ Dinner: _____ Snack: _____
SATURDAY Breakfast: _____ Lunch: _____ Dinner: _____ Snack: _____	**SUNDAY** Breakfast: _____ Lunch: _____ Dinner: _____ Snack: _____

SHOPPING LIST:

For the month of: _____

Week of: ⚜	**MONDAY** Breakfast: _____ Lunch: _____ Dinner: _____ Snack: _____
TUESDAY Breakfast: _____ Lunch: _____ Dinner: _____ Snack: _____	**WEDNESDAY** Breakfast: _____ Lunch: _____ Dinner: _____ Snack: _____
THURSDAY Breakfast: _____ Lunch: _____ Dinner: _____ Snack: _____	**FRIDAY** Breakfast: _____ Lunch: _____ Dinner: _____ Snack: _____
SATURDAY Breakfast: _____ Lunch: _____ Dinner: _____ Snack: _____	**SUNDAY** Breakfast: _____ Lunch: _____ Dinner: _____ Snack: _____

SHOPPING LIST:

_____ _____
_____ _____
_____ _____
_____ _____
_____ _____
_____ _____

For the month of: _____

Week of: _____

MONDAY
Breakfast: _____
Lunch: _____
Dinner: _____
Snack: _____

TUESDAY
Breakfast: _____
Lunch: _____
Dinner: _____
Snack: _____

WEDNESDAY
Breakfast: _____
Lunch: _____
Dinner: _____
Snack: _____

THURSDAY
Breakfast: _____
Lunch: _____
Dinner: _____
Snack: _____

FRIDAY
Breakfast: _____
Lunch: _____
Dinner: _____
Snack: _____

SATURDAY
Breakfast: _____
Lunch: _____
Dinner: _____
Snack: _____

SUNDAY
Breakfast: _____
Lunch: _____
Dinner: _____
Snack: _____

SHOPPING LIST:

_____   _____
_____   _____
_____   _____
_____   _____
_____   _____
_____   _____

For the month of: _____

Week of:

MONDAY
Breakfast: _____
Lunch: _____
Dinner: _____
Snack: _____

TUESDAY
Breakfast: _____
Lunch: _____
Dinner: _____
Snack: _____

WEDNESDAY
Breakfast: _____
Lunch: _____
Dinner: _____
Snack: _____

THURSDAY
Breakfast: _____
Lunch: _____
Dinner: _____
Snack: _____

FRIDAY
Breakfast: _____
Lunch: _____
Dinner: _____
Snack: _____

SATURDAY
Breakfast: _____
Lunch: _____
Dinner: _____
Snack: _____

SUNDAY
Breakfast: _____
Lunch: _____
Dinner: _____
Snack: _____

SHOPPING LIST:

For the month of: _____

Week of:	MONDAY
	Breakfast: _____
	Lunch: _____
	Dinner: _____
	Snack: _____

TUESDAY	WEDNESDAY
Breakfast: _____	Breakfast: _____
Lunch: _____	Lunch: _____
Dinner: _____	Dinner: _____
Snack: _____	Snack: _____

THURSDAY	FRIDAY
Breakfast: _____	Breakfast: _____
Lunch: _____	Lunch: _____
Dinner: _____	Dinner: _____
Snack: _____	Snack: _____

SATURDAY	SUNDAY
Breakfast: _____	Breakfast: _____
Lunch: _____	Lunch: _____
Dinner: _____	Dinner: _____
Snack: _____	Snack: _____

SHOPPING LIST:

_____ _____
_____ _____
_____ _____
_____ _____
_____ _____
_____ _____
_____ _____

For the month of: _____

Week of:	**MONDAY**
	Breakfast: _____
	Lunch: _____
	Dinner: _____
	Snack: _____

TUESDAY	**WEDNESDAY**
Breakfast: _____	Breakfast: _____
Lunch: _____	Lunch: _____
Dinner: _____	Dinner: _____
Snack: _____	Snack: _____

THURSDAY	**FRIDAY**
Breakfast: _____	Breakfast: _____
Lunch: _____	Lunch: _____
Dinner: _____	Dinner: _____
Snack: _____	Snack: _____

SATURDAY	**SUNDAY**
Breakfast: _____	Breakfast: _____
Lunch: _____	Lunch: _____
Dinner: _____	Dinner: _____
Snack: _____	Snack: _____

SHOPPING LIST:

_____   _____
_____   _____
_____   _____
_____   _____
_____   _____
_____   _____

For the month of: _____

Week of:	**MONDAY** Breakfast: _____ Lunch: _____ Dinner: _____ Snack: _____
TUESDAY Breakfast: _____ Lunch: _____ Dinner: _____ Snack: _____	**WEDNESDAY** Breakfast: _____ Lunch: _____ Dinner: _____ Snack: _____
THURSDAY Breakfast: _____ Lunch: _____ Dinner: _____ Snack: _____	**FRIDAY** Breakfast: _____ Lunch: _____ Dinner: _____ Snack: _____
SATURDAY Breakfast: _____ Lunch: _____ Dinner: _____ Snack: _____	**SUNDAY** Breakfast: _____ Lunch: _____ Dinner: _____ Snack: _____

SHOPPING LIST:

For the month of: _____

Week of:

MONDAY
Breakfast: _____
_____
Lunch: _____
_____
Dinner: _____
_____
Snack: _____

TUESDAY
Breakfast: _____
_____
Lunch: _____
_____
Dinner: _____
_____
Snack: _____

WEDNESDAY
Breakfast: _____
_____
Lunch: _____
_____
Dinner: _____
_____
Snack: _____

THURSDAY
Breakfast: _____
_____
Lunch: _____
_____
Dinner: _____
_____
Snack: _____

FRIDAY
Breakfast: _____
_____
Lunch: _____
_____
Dinner: _____
_____
Snack: _____

SATURDAY
Breakfast: _____
_____
Lunch: _____
_____
Dinner: _____
_____
Snack: _____

SUNDAY
Breakfast: _____
_____
Lunch: _____
_____
Dinner: _____
_____
Snack: _____

SHOPPING LIST:

_____   _____
_____   _____
_____   _____
_____   _____
_____   _____
_____   _____

For the month of: _____

Week of: _____

MONDAY
Breakfast: _____

Lunch: _____

Dinner: _____

Snack: _____

TUESDAY
Breakfast: _____

Lunch: _____

Dinner: _____

Snack: _____

WEDNESDAY
Breakfast: _____

Lunch: _____

Dinner: _____

Snack: _____

THURSDAY
Breakfast: _____

Lunch: _____

Dinner: _____

Snack: _____

FRIDAY
Breakfast: _____

Lunch: _____

Dinner: _____

Snack: _____

SATURDAY
Breakfast: _____

Lunch: _____

Dinner: _____

Snack: _____

SUNDAY
Breakfast: _____

Lunch: _____

Dinner: _____

Snack: _____

SHOPPING LIST:

For the month of: _____

Week of:

MONDAY
Breakfast: _____
_____
Lunch: _____
_____
Dinner: _____
_____
Snack: _____

TUESDAY
Breakfast: _____
_____
Lunch: _____
_____
Dinner: _____
_____
Snack: _____

WEDNESDAY
Breakfast: _____
_____
Lunch: _____
_____
Dinner: _____
_____
Snack: _____

THURSDAY
Breakfast: _____
_____
Lunch: _____
_____
Dinner: _____
_____
Snack: _____

FRIDAY
Breakfast: _____
_____
Lunch: _____
_____
Dinner: _____
_____
Snack: _____

SATURDAY
Breakfast: _____
_____
Lunch: _____
_____
Dinner: _____
_____
Snack: _____

SUNDAY
Breakfast: _____
_____
Lunch: _____
_____
Dinner: _____
_____
Snack: _____

SHOPPING LIST:

For the month of: _____

Week of:	**MONDAY**
	Breakfast: _____
	Lunch: _____
	Dinner: _____
	Snack: _____

TUESDAY	**WEDNESDAY**
Breakfast: _____	Breakfast: _____
Lunch: _____	Lunch: _____
Dinner: _____	Dinner: _____
Snack: _____	Snack: _____

THURSDAY	**FRIDAY**
Breakfast: _____	Breakfast: _____
Lunch: _____	Lunch: _____
Dinner: _____	Dinner: _____
Snack: _____	Snack: _____

SATURDAY	**SUNDAY**
Breakfast: _____	Breakfast: _____
Lunch: _____	Lunch: _____
Dinner: _____	Dinner: _____
Snack: _____	Snack: _____

SHOPPING LIST:

CPSIA information can be obtained
at www.ICGtesting.com
Printed in the USA
LVHW03s0903230718
584632LV00009B/341/P